Martin Luther

Judith O'Neill

Published in cooperation with Cambridge University Press
Lerner Publications Company · Minneapolis

Editors' Note: In preparing this edition of *The Cambridge Topic Books* for publication, the editors have made only a few minor changes in the original material. In some isolated cases, British spelling and usage were altered in order to avoid possible confusion for our readers. Whenever necessary, information was added to clarify references to people, places, and events in British history. An index was also provided in each volume.

LIBRARY OF CONGRESS CATALOGING IN PUBLICATION DATA

O'Neill, Judith.
    Martin Luther.

    (A Cambridge Topic Book)
    Includes index.
    SUMMARY: Presents the life and philosophy of a key figure in the Protestant Reformation.

    1. Luther, Martin, 1483-1546—Juvenile literature. 2. Reformation—Germany—Biography—Juvenile literature. [1. Luther, Martin, 1483-1546. 2. Reformers. 3. Reformation] I. Title.

BR325.064 1979   230'.4'10924 [B] [92]   78-56804
ISBN 0-8225-1215-7

This edition first published 1979 by Lerner Publications Company
by permission of Cambridge University Press.

Original edition copyright © 1975 by Cambridge University Press
as part of *The Cambridge Introduction to the History of Mankind: Topic Book*.

International Standard Book Number: 0-8225-1215-7
Library of Congress Catalog Card Number: 78-56804

Manufactured in the United States of America.

This edition is available exclusively from:
Lerner Publications Company, 241 First Avenue North, Minneapolis, Minnesota 55401

East West Sewing Co. $4.95 7/79 20661

Contents

1 How can we find out the truth about Martin Luther?

Martin Luther, painted by his friend Lucas Cranach in 1528. Lucas Cranach (1472–1553) painted Luther and his friends and members of his family. He also made propaganda woodcuts for some of Luther's pamphlets and designed some of the pictures to illustrate Luther's German Bible. As Cranach grew older, much of his work was carried out by his sons Hans and Lucas or by other craftsmen in his workshop. Sometimes we cannot be quite sure how much was done by the older artist himself and how much was done by his son Lucas.

Martin Luther lived and died in Germany more than four hundred years ago. The things he did and said and the books he wrote were so important that all of us today are still affected by them. Nothing in Europe was ever quite the same after Luther. Not only did the Western Church divide into two parts, the Catholic and the Protestant, but people's everyday life in town and village, church and school, was gradually changed by Luther's ideas and by the Reformation movement he led.

Luckily for us, there is plenty of material for historians working on Luther to use. He wrote lots of letters which we still have. He wrote books and pamphlets that have been reprinted over and over again and are still in our libraries today. He gave sermons and lectures about the Bible. His students used to take notes at these lectures and we still have some of those students' notebooks. He loved to sit at table and talk to his family and friends as they ate dinner together. Some of his students were always busily jotting down everything Luther said; this is called his *Table Talk* and we can still read that today too. Luther and his family were painted several times by his friend Lucas Cranach. These portraits show us what Luther looked like. Other German artists – Dürer, the Holbeins, Grünewald – tell us about the kind of people who lived in Luther's world. Their religious paintings help us to understand how people felt about religion. We can even look at old plays, like the English morality play *Everyman* and its Flemish counterpart *Elckerlyc*, to see how ordinary people thought about God at the end of the fifteenth century when Martin Luther was a boy.

You may think that with all this 'evidence', as historians call it, we should find it easy to decide what Luther was like and what he thought and did. But it is not as easy as it looks. Even when Luther was still alive, people could not agree about what he was like. Some thought he was a great and good man sent by God to make the Church better. Others thought he was a *right:* The Crucifixion, painted by the German artist Mathis Grünewald (1470–1528) for the altarpiece at Isenheim. Many of Grünewald's paintings reflect intense concentration on the agony of Christ, shown here in the strained hands and the stretched body. Luther would probably have seen paintings like this one as he was growing up.

wicked man who tried to destroy the Church. Over the centuries people have gone on arguing about Luther. Some have said he was kind and jolly, witty and loving; others have said he was vain and greedy, rude and spiteful. It is very hard to get at the truth. Today things are becoming a bit clearer. Protestant historians are beginning to admit Luther's weaknesses and mistakes; Catholic historians are beginning to admit that many of Luther's criticisms of the Church were right. So if we take the trouble to look at Luther's own writings and conversations and if we listen patiently to the views of different historians, we can gradually piece together a fairly true picture of this extraordinary man.

Two different views of Martin Luther. On the left is a woodcut of Luther as his enemies saw him — a seven-headed monster. On the right is a painting of Luther as his friends and followers saw him. Moses is on the far left with the books of the Law (the Ten Commandments etc.). Then comes John the Baptist; in the full picture from which this detail is taken he is pointing up to Christ on the cross. Next there is a self-portrait of the artist himself, Lucas Cranach. Finally comes Martin Luther, pointing to the words of the New Testament. Cranach painted the picture for an altarpiece in Weimar.

Four of the artists whose pictures appear in this book — Cranach, Grünewald, Dürer and Burgkmair — were all born at about the same time. Hans Holbein was born about twenty years later. The lives of all five overlapped with that of Martin Luther.

2 Luther's childhood

Martin Luther was born just before midnight on 10 November 1483 in Eisleben in Thuringian Saxony. The next morning was St Martin's Day so he was taken to church and baptised with the name Martin. His father, Hans Luther, had been a peasant working on the land but the year after Martin was born the whole family moved to the mining area of Mansfeld. Here Hans began work as a copper miner. He did so well for himself that before long he could rent some smelting furnaces attached to the mine and employ other men to work for him. On the Mansfeld town council he acted as spokesman for the people in his parish. Hans Luther became a respected citizen.

Very much later in his life, Martin Luther said, 'I am the son of a peasant. My great-grandfather, my grandfather and my father were peasants... Then my father moved to Mansfeld where he became a miner.' You can see here how Luther wanted to make it clear that he belonged to the common people and was not born into the wealthy classes. He rather overlooked the fact that his father had left the peasant's life and even the miner's life behind him and had become a prosperous employer who counted for something in the little community of Mansfeld.

Luther goes to school

Luther's parents wanted to give him a good education. They could see that he was very intelligent and so they hoped he would become a successful lawyer. Then he would probably be able to marry a rich woman, live a comfortable life, and provide for his parents in their old age.

Martin first went to school when he was seven years old to the small local 'Latin school' at Mansfeld. He stayed here until he was fourteen, learning how to read and write Latin and even how to speak it fluently. This was very important because Latin was used not only by the Church for its services and laws but by

lawyers, diplomats, astronomers, doctors and school teachers. Indeed if a boy wanted to go into any profession he had to be fluent in Latin. At Mansfeld Martin would also have learned to recite the Ten Commandments and the Apostles' Creed, but there was no arithmetic or history. All the boys had to learn their lessons by heart and recite them to the teacher. If they made a mistake or if they forgot to speak in Latin all the time and lapsed into German, they were punished with a cane. Luther remembered how once he was 'caned fifteen times in a single morning'!

Luther's father, Hans, and his mother, Margaretha, painted by Lucas Cranach in about 1527 when they were visiting their son in Wittenberg. Hans Luther died in 1530, and his wife in 1531.

A German schoolmaster's signboard painted by Hans Holbein the younger (1498–1543). The picture shows how boys and girls were taught individually.

Magdeburg and Eisenach

When he was fourteen, Martin moved to a larger and better school in Magdeburg where he stayed for one year. This may have been the cathedral choir school. Certainly he learned to take part in the liturgical singing in the cathedral services. Magdeburg was a long way from Mansfeld so Martin lived in lodgings and came home to his family at the end of the year. His new school was conducted by a religious order called the 'Brothers of the Common Life'. The Brothers put great emphasis on a warm personal faith in God and on a sound knowledge of the Bible. Both of these were to be very important for Luther all through his life.

Finally, when he was fifteen, Martin went to his third school, this time in Eisenach, and he stayed there for two years. He liked this school best of all. It was a happy time and he always looked back with affection to 'the dear old town of Eisenach'. He lived with the family of Frau Ursula Cotta. The story is that she heard him singing in the church choir and was so taken with his voice that she offered him lodgings in her own house. He had his meals each day with Frau Cotta's brother, a wealthy merchant called Schalbe. In return for his meals he took the merchant's little boy to and from school and helped him with his homework. Martin often joined with other boys and went round the town singing carols outside people's houses in the hope of earning a little money.

Martin was very fond of Trebonius, the scholarly headmaster of the Eisenach school. He used to recall how Trebonius would come into the classroom and take off his hat respectfully to the boys before he sat down. 'Who knows', Trebonius would say, 'which of these young students may one day be a worshipful mayor, or a doctor, or a chancellor, or even a great ruler?'

Luther and his father

Some historians have suggested that all through these later years at school and even more at the university, Martin felt a strong need to have his father's approval for everything he did. They think that he used to feel very anxious and unhappy whenever his father was angry with him and that this fear of his father may well have affected his feelings about God. He certainly tended to see God at this time as a stern and even

This gilt copper reliquary in the shape of a gabled shrine was made in Augsburg about 1520. It contained the relics of a saint — some of his bones perhaps or a piece of his clothing. Reliquaries were often carried in the processions at religious festivals. The relics of saints were objects of devotion.
right: Plague-stricken pilgrims appeal to the Virgin Mary at her shrine at Regensberg. Woodcut by Michael Oestendorfer, 1520.

angry father whose approval he must always try to earn by being good. Other historians argue that there is no evidence at all for this excessive fear of his father. They say that in fact Luther got on well with him and that his feelings about God were not based on his own private fears but were shared by most people at that time. You will see evidence for this if you read a play like *Everyman*. God was thought of as a stern judge who would punish sinners, rather than as a loving and forgiving father. Nevertheless, it does seem that Luther's fear and even terror of God's anger were more intense than most people's. Perhaps his relationship with his father had something to do with this.

Everyday life in the Church

Apart from his schools and his family, the most important influence on Luther as he was growing up was the life of the church. He went to mass with his parents on Sundays when he was at home in Mansfeld. At Magdeburg and Eisenach he sang in the church choir. The prayers and Bible readings in church were all in Latin. Martin could understand them but many people had no idea what they were about. They took more notice of the bright statues and windows that showed them the lives of Jesus and the saints. At mass the priest stood at the altar with his back to the people and offered first the bread and then the wine to God as a sacrifice. The people would hear him say Jesus's words 'This is my body...' and 'This is the cup of my blood.' Everyone would join in the Lord's Prayer in Latin

but there were no hymns for the people as the choir did all the singing. On Corpus Christi and other feast days, Martin and his friends would have a holiday. Then they could watch the colourful processions going through the streets, with the priests carrying a statue of the Virgin Mary or St Anne or St Elizabeth. They could watch the townsfolk acting in Biblical plays on carts that were pulled from one street corner to the next. On fast days, like Ash Wednesday and Good Friday, Martin and his family and friends would eat very little food, to remind themselves of Jesus's suffering and death. In all these ways, on Sundays, feasts and fasts, religion was a familiar and important part of Martin's everyday life.

3 Brother Martin

When Martin Luther was seventeen years old, in 1501, he went to the university at Erfurt. Here he studied first Latin, logic and philosophy. Then he moved on to geometry, arithmetic, music, astronomy and more philosophy. It was a strict life of study and prayer with set times for lectures and reading and a set time for going to bed at night. For relaxation Luther played the lute and enjoyed singing with his student friends as they sat drinking beer in the evenings. He was expecting to become a lawyer as his father had hoped. Then suddenly, soon after he had taken his Master's degree in 1505, when he was twenty-one years old, his whole life changed direction. He decided to give up all idea of being a lawyer and of marrying a rich wife. He was going to become a friar instead. He did not ask his father's advice and in fact his father was furious when he found out. Martin simply had a farewell meal with his friends and then entered the monastery of the Augustinian friars at Erfurt.

Thirty-five years later Luther said that he had become a friar because he had been frightened by a stroke of lightning in a storm and in his terror had promised St Anne to enter a religious order if she would save his life. Like many of the things Luther said when he was an old man, we cannot be quite sure about this. He often forgot how things had really happened. Nevertheless, whether it was the stroke of lightning that made him take this decision or not, we can be sure that Luther became a friar 'not freely but walled around with the terror and agony of sudden death'. His intense fear of God's punishment after death had made him give up ordinary life in the world to live as a friar because he believed – as did everyone else – that a friar's or a monk's life was more holy and more pleasing to God than a layman's life. He deliberately chose a strict community rather than an easy-going one and he tried very hard to keep the rules well. 'If ever a monk got to heaven through monasticism', he said later, 'I should have

Martin Luther as an Augustinian friar, engraved by Cranach in 1520.

been that man.' (We often find Luther referred to – by himself and others – as a *monk*, even though he was, strictly speaking, a *friar*. This is because there was not a great deal of difference between monks and friars by Luther's day, though they had originally been very different.)

Monastery at Erfurt

The full name of the monastery Luther chose to enter was the Reformed Congregation of the Eremetical Order of St Augustine. This order of Augustinian friars (or Austin friars, as the English called them) had been founded in 1243 and two hundred years later, when it had grown lax, some of the houses (including the one at Erfurt) had been 'reformed'. This meant that they followed their monastic rule very strictly. John Staupitz, soon to become a good friend to Martin Luther, was the Vicar-General of these reformed or observant houses.

The city of Erfurt where Luther became an Augustinian friar. This engraving is from the Nuremberg Chronicle of 1493.

There were seventy friars in the Erfurt house when Luther joined, half of them priests. Priests and brothers were all expected to work hard and to spend long hours in prayer. The Augustinian friars were a begging order and all the members had to take a turn at going out in the streets to beg for money or food. The order also put great emphasis on the study of theology so Luther knew he would be able to continue his reading and thinking about the Bible. Some of the more brilliant friars were asked to become professors in the universities. Both the strict poverty of the order and its tradition of scholarship appealed to Luther. Like all the other friars he wore the black cowl and a long white strip of cloth hanging from the shoulders to the feet to represent the yoke of Christ. Like all the other friars his head was shaved to the usual tonsure – a fringe of hair around the bald head to represent Jesus's crown of thorns.

It is worth trying to understand why Luther was drawn to the life of a religious community. Luther did not see the monastery as an escape from the world or as a useless way of

life. We have seen how members of his order did come out into the world to beg, teach or preach. But whether they stayed within the four walls of the monastery or came out to take up duties in the world, all these friars believed that by rejecting the hope of a comfortable home, a well-paid job, a wife and children, freedom to come and go, they would be better able to offer themselves to God. Luther felt that by giving himself to God in prayer and self-sacrifice he would make sure of his salvation. He thought he could be more sure that when he came to the end of his life and faced the moment of God's judgement, God would save him from hell and reward him with heaven if he had given up worldly pleasures to become a friar.

At first all went well for Luther in the monastery but as time went by he began to be very troubled and unhappy. He felt he was 'dust and ashes and full of sin'. He would confess his sins again and again to a priest, even for hours on end, but when he came away he was always afraid he had left out some forgotten sin or that he was not really sorry enough about the things he had done wrong. When he was ordained as a priest himself in

1507 and celebrated his first mass he was overwhelmed by a dreadful sense of his own guilt. He was still terrified that God would be angry with him and punish him. This does not mean that Luther was really bad or that his sins were any worse than the other friars'. What we have to grasp with our imagination if we are ever to understand Luther is the terrible anguish and suffering he went through during those years. He was constantly overcome by his sense of sinfulness, his terror of God's punishment and his utter despair of ever living a perfect life that would please God. However hard he tried, Luther could find no escape, no comfort, no hope.

Luther goes to Wittenberg

In 1509, when Luther was twenty-six, he was moved from the Augustinian monastery in Erfurt to the Augustinian monastery in Wittenberg. Wittenberg was in Saxony, one of the three hundred or so states (some of them very small indeed) which together made up the Holy Roman Empire. The Holy Roman Empire was really the German Empire. It had been set up seven centuries earlier and claimed to be a continuation of the ancient Roman empire. Each of the major states within the Empire was governed by a prince. Seven of these princes elected the Emperor to rule over the whole Empire. These seven princes were known as Electors (see maps on the next page).

In Luther's time the Emperor was Maximilian I, succeeded in 1519 by his grandson Charles V, who was already King of Spain. Both these Emperors were members of the powerful Habsburg family which was gaining a monopoly of the emperorship. All through his reign, Charles V was to be busy with wars against France on one hand and resistance to the Ottoman Turks on the other. His concern with these international troubles and his long absences

The Last Judgement by Albrecht Dürer (1471–1528). Most of Dürer's great pictures are wood or copper engravings rather than paintings. In this woodcut, made in 1509 or 1510, Jesus Christ is seen as the Judge, with His feet on the round earth to symbolize His power over the whole world: perhaps the figures of the man and the woman kneeling in front of Him are Everyman and Everywoman. In the centre of the picture the dead are rising from their graves on the day of judgement; on the left, angels are ushering the saved towards the blazing light of heaven; on the right, winged devils hustle the damned into the jaws of hell.

Europe in 1500

Legend:
— Boundary of Holy Roman Empire
— National boundaries
▨ Habsburg States

0 km 150
0 miles 100

The Holy Roman Empire c. 1500

Legend:
— Boundary of Holy Roman Empire
⋯ Boundaries of some of the larger states

0 50 100km
0 50 100 miles

from his German territories partly explain why he did not do much to deal with the crisis in the Church soon to be set off by Luther. Saxony itself was ruled by the Elector Frederick the Wise. As we shall see, Frederick's firm support for Luther and later the support of his successors, the Electors John and John Frederick, as well as the support of other German princes, had a good deal to do with Luther's success and with the spread of the Reformation.

The visit to Rome

Luther had been sent to Wittenberg to lecture in philosophy at the university there. Wittenberg was a dull little town of about two thousand people and the university was a very new one, less than ten years old. After the pleasant gardens of Erfurt, Luther found Wittenberg very depressing. He was moved back to Erfurt for a time and then, in about 1510, he was asked to go to Rome to deal with some business arising from a dispute

A portrait of Frederick the Wise, Elector of Saxony, by Dürer. Frederick's sympathy and protection helped Luther when his life was in danger. Notice the intricately slashed sleeves of Frederick's velvet doublet.

St Peter's Square and the Vatican in 1520. The rebuilding of St Peter's basilica began in 1506, about four years before Luther's visit to Rome, and it went on for more than a hundred years. The Vatican is the Pope's residence.

within his order. (The Augustinians were directly under their head in Rome and so difficult problems had to be taken there for a decision.) A visit or a pilgrimage to Rome, the holy centre of Christendom, was a great event for any friar or monk. Luther went off full of hope, crossing the Alps on foot, and when he saw the great city in the distance he knelt on the ground and cried 'Hail, Holy Rome!' But when he arrived he was sadly disappointed. He later said that he had 'gone to Rome with onions but had come back with garlic'. He said he had been shocked at the way the Italian priests gabbled through the services as quickly as they could. These priests laughed at him

for taking the mass seriously. He was amazed at the life of luxury many of them lived and was sad to see that often they did not bother to keep their vows at all.

The great St Peter's basilica was being rebuilt but there were many other churches that pilgrims could visit and Luther went from one to another. As the custom was, he prayed by the relics of saints who had died or been martyred long ago. Relics were the bones or perhaps fragments of clothing that had belonged to the saint. No one could be too sure how genuine these relics were but great value was attached to them. 'I was such a simple-minded pilgrim', Luther said later, 'that I

A group of German pilgrims in front of the basilica of Santa Croce (Holy Cross) in Rome. They are equipped for long journeying and there seems to be a local guide showing them the sights. We know that Luther saw this church on his visit. This picture is part of a much larger one painted by Hans Burgkmair (1473–1531) in 1514, about four years after Luther's visit.

The creation of man, painted by Michelangelo (1475–1564), on the ceiling of the Sistine Chapel in the Vatican. Although Luther is not likely to have seen it during his visit, Michelangelo was actually working then on this famous ceiling. Such work of the great Renaissance artists of Italy may have seemed more classical than religious to a man accustomed to German pictures.

believed everything I saw and was shown.' Like all the other pilgrims, he went up 'Pilate's Stairs' near the Lateran basilica. He went on his hands and knees, saying the prayer 'Our Father. . .' at every step. His hope was that each time he said this prayer on the stairs, God would reduce the time his grandfather's soul had to stay in purgatory by one year. (Purgatory was an intermediate state between this world and heaven. The Church taught that after death Christians would spend a long period in purgatory, being finally cleansed of their sins by fire to make them fit for heaven. You will find out more about this in Chapter 5, on Indulgences.) When at last Luther reached the top of the stairs, he had a moment of great doubt. 'Who knows if it is really true?' he said. He began to question whether it was really true that God wanted people to 'earn' their own salvation, or the salvation of their friends and relations, by visiting shrines, praying near relics, paying money, or climbing up stairs on their hands and knees. That sudden moment of doubt was very important in Luther's thinking about the Christian faith.

4 Professor at Wittenberg

When Martin Luther came back from Rome he was soon transferred again from Erfurt to Wittenberg. Here he was able to talk a good deal with his friend and confessor, John Staupitz, the Vicar-General of the Augustinians in Saxony. Staupitz was a fine scholar and a wise and sympathetic pastor. He knew Martin well already and had often tried to comfort and reassure him when he was unhappy about his sins or terrified by God. Luther and Staupitz remained close friends right to the end of Staupitz's life in spite of many disagreements between them. 'Staupitz was my first father in this teaching', said Luther, 'and he bore me in Christ.'

As Staupitz was getting old he wanted to retire from his job as professor of Biblical theology in the university at Wittenberg and he persuaded Martin Luther to take it on. In 1512 Luther graduated as Doctor of Theology at a splendid ceremony when he promised that all through his life he would preach the Bible and help people to understand it. He was installed as professor of theology at the age of twenty-eight and so began the work that he was to go on doing all through his life with very few breaks – the job of lecturing twice a week for thirty years to many generations of students. He loved theology and much preferred it to philosophy. 'Theology', he

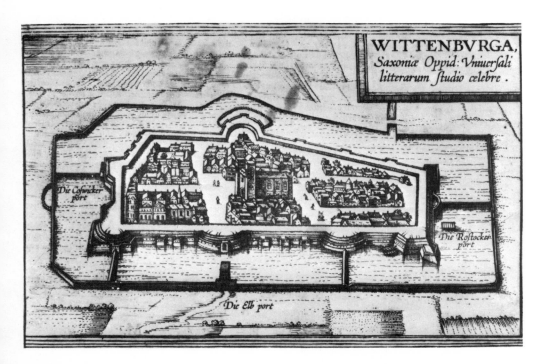

WITTENBVRGA,
Saxoniæ Oppid: Vniuerſali litterarum ſtudio celebre.

Die Coſwicker port

Die Roſtocker port

Die Elb port

The university town of Wittenberg as seen in a late-sixteenth-century engraving. In the centre is the church where Luther nailed up his Ninety-five Theses. The town seems to consist of compact clumps of houses between the main streets, and has a public well not far from the church.

The church where Luther nailed up the Theses still stands today. It is called the Schlosskirche or Castle Church.

said, 'searches out the nut from the shell, the kernel from the grain, and the marrow from the bones.'

Luther's first lectures were about the Psalms. Then he went on to lecture on two of St Paul's letters — the Letter to the Romans and the Letter to the Galatians. He had learned Greek and Hebrew over the past few years so that he could read the Old and New Testaments in the languages they were originally written in instead of in the Latin translation — the Vulgate — that most people used.

Luther thought of a good idea to help the students take notes at his lectures. He had special copies of the Bible printed with very wide spaces between each line, and he gave one of these Bibles to each student. Then, as Luther lectured on each verse of Psalms or of Romans, the students could write down the points they wanted to remember in the space between the right lines. Luther's lectures were very popular and students crowded in to hear him. This is how one of them remembered him. 'He was a man of middle stature, with a voice which combined sharpness and softness. It was soft in tone, sharp in the enunciation of syllables, words and sentences. He spoke neither too quickly nor too slowly, but at an even pace without hesitation and very clearly.'

Luther discovers the 'gateway to paradise'

Perhaps it was while he was working away on Romans for these Wittenberg lectures or perhaps it was a year or two earlier or later when Luther made a great discovery. It was a turning point in his life. As he read Romans he was still struggling with his terrible fear of God. In Chapter 1, verse 17, he read 'In the gospel the righteousness of God is shown through faith for faith . . . . He who is righteous through faith shall live.' Luther hated that phrase 'the righteousness of God' — the 'justice of God' as it is sometimes translated. He hated it because he thought it meant that God's kind of justice was harsh and unforgiving. He saw God's justice as punishing men for their sin. He knew that however hard he tried he could never be perfectly good and could not help sinning. So he could see nothing ahead of him but God's justice, God's punishment. He was so afraid of God that he hated Him. 'I did not love, indeed I hated this just God who punished sinners', he wrote.

Then one day, as he read over and over again that verse from Romans – 'he who is righteous through faith shall live' – he suddenly began to see it differently. He saw that what Paul meant was not that Christians have to try harder and harder to be good but that if they really have faith in God and trust in Him, God will give them His *own* goodness, His *own* righteousness. If a man will have faith in God, God will regard him as good in spite of his sins. Only God, of course, can give man faith in the first place – 'no one can give himself faith' said Luther. So both man's faith and God's righteousness are free gifts of God and cannot possibly be earned by good deeds or by fasting or by giving money to the poor or even by saying prayers or receiving the sacraments of the Church. Anyone who trusts in God through Jesus Christ need have no fear. God is sure to save him.

This was Luther's great moment of discovery. He said later, 'It seemed to me as if I had been born again and as if I had entered paradise through newly opened doors. All at once the Bible began to speak in quite a different way to me... The very phrase "the righteousness of God", which I had hated before, was the one that now I loved the best of all. That is how that passage of Paul's became for me the gateway to paradise.'

Now at last Luther felt free. His terror of God had gone. He felt he had grasped the Christian gospel properly for the first time in his life. He now saw himself – and every Christian – as 'always a sinner, always sorry for his sins, always right with God'. For Luther, the key to this new freedom was Jesus

The Great Dance of Death was a common theme in the fifteenth and sixteenth centuries. Its purpose was to show that all men of all classes must eventually face death. This woodcut is from a series by Holbein, published 1523/4, and shows a monk being dragged unwillingly away from his worldly wealth.

Christ Himself and the death and resurrection of Jesus Christ. When Luther talks about 'faith' he means faith in the God who comes to men in Jesus Christ. He means that if men want to know what God is like and how He acts and how He feels about men, then they must turn to Jesus Christ. This is the faith that stood at the centre of Luther's life.

Now that Luther was free he wanted to share his great discovery with everyone else in the Church. That is where he began to run into trouble.

5 Indulgences

Luther was not only a professor in the university. He was also a preacher in the parish church of Wittenberg and every Sunday the church was full of people who had come to hear him. He was busy in all sorts of other ways too. This is a letter he wrote to his friend, John Lang, in 1516. 'I need two secretaries because I do almost nothing all day long but write letters. . . I am lecturer in the cloister, reader at meals, preach daily and direct the students' studies; I am the Prior's vicar (which means being vicar eleven times over!), inspector of fish ponds at Leitzkau . . . and expounder of St Paul and the Psalms, besides my letter writing.'

Now that he had broken through his fears to a new and confident trust in God, Luther began to look in a fresh and critical way at some of the practices of the Church. In particular, he was disturbed by the growing abuse of indulgences. An indulgence, in Luther's time, was generally a certificate granted by the Pope in return for the payment of a fee to the Church. This certificate stated that the soul of the dead relative or friend of the purchaser would have his time in purgatory reduced by many years or cancelled altogether. However it is worth looking back well before Luther's time to see how indulgences first arose and why the Church had introduced them.

Indulgences to avoid the shame of public penance

We have to begin by looking first at the sacrament of penance, one of the seven sacraments of the Catholic Church. The Church believed – and still believes – that Jesus had given to Peter and the other apostles and through them to the priests of the Church the power to 'bind and loose' – that is the power to give or withhold God's forgiveness. This forgiveness was passed on to Christians through the sacrament of penance.

Penance had three parts – contrition, confession and satisfaction. First you had to be really sorry for what you had done wrong (contrition); then you had to tell a priest what you had done wrong (confession); the priest would then declare that you were forgiven by God (absolution); finally he would give you some punishment to undergo – something to show God that you were really sorry (satisfaction). In the case of small sins the punishment was never very great – perhaps you would have to say some prayers, or do without butter or eggs for a day, or give some money to the poor. By about the tenth century however the Church had worked out a system of *public* penances for people who had committed very serious sins – murder, for example. After the usual contrition, confession and absolution, these sinners then had to go through a 'satisfaction' that often lasted for years. It generally meant that they were not allowed to come into church for mass or to receive the sacraments but had to sit outside dressed in sackcloth. Everyone could see them and would know what they had done wrong. The whole thing was very embarrassing. The suggestion then arose that these people could get out of their public penance if they were prepared to pay a large sum of money to the Church. The Church generally used the money to care for the sick or to build new churches. This was the real beginning of indulgences. The indulgence was the certificate issued by the Pope (or sometimes by the bishop) to let the sinner off his public penance in return for a fee. It did not let people off the contrition and confession parts of penance; it was simply a substitute for the satisfaction part, after the priest had given absolution.

Indulgences to avoid punishment in purgatory

Now between the tenth and the fifteenth centuries the use

Selling the indulgences. This woodcut is by Jörg Breu (1475–1537) who worked in Augsburg from 1502 onwards. The Pope's document authorizing the sale is hanging on a pole, festooned with seals. Clergy are present, but the money is being handled by laymen, equipped with scales and iron-bound chest.

of indulgences gradually became much more complicated. Indulgences came to be sold not just for letting people off punishments in *this* world but also for letting people off punishments in purgatory. The Church taught that when you died, even though you were sorry for your sins and had already done a good deal of 'satisfaction' for them on earth, there would still be more punishment to be undergone before you were really fit to live with God in heaven. The completing of this punishment was to be done in the fires of purgatory where souls would spend hundreds of days or years being finally cleansed or 'purged' of their sins. (The Church did not mean *literal* years – purgatory was outside measured time.) Naturally enough, no one looked forward to these 'years' in purgatory and people were glad to have the chance to buy an indulgence – to pay money to the Church in this life in return for being let off some or all of these punishments after death.

This practice of granting indulgences to lessen or cancel the time in purgatory may have first arisen in the eleventh century when Christians were fighting Muslims in the Crusades. Muslims believed that the souls of their soldiers killed in battle went straight to heaven; the souls of the Christians however (according to the Church's teaching) went first to purgatory. The fear of years in purgatory after sudden death in battle discouraged Christians from going to the Crusades and there was a serious shortage of soldiers. The Popes of that time began to grant indulgences to give a complete cancelling of all punishment in purgatory to any soldiers who were killed in the Crusades and even to those who simply fought in the Crusades. Then, between the twelfth and the fifteenth centuries, these indulgences were extended from soldiers who fought the Muslims to any other people who would pay the proper fee. This was a time when the Church was in urgent need of money and indulgences provided a steady source of income.

The treasury of merit

Why was it that the Church believed it had the power to cancel a soul's sufferings in purgatory? The theologians explained it this way: the Church had control over the 'treasury of merit' – a kind of spiritual 'bank' in heaven where the merit earned by the good deeds and holy lives of the saints was stored. The

Pope could take merit from this treasury and give it to a sinner who needed it and who had paid for an indulgence. In this way the saints in heaven could help the sinners on earth or in purgatory.

Indulgences for people who had already died

The final development of indulgences came in the late fifteenth century when it became possible to buy an indulgence on behalf of someone who was already dead. In this way you could shorten the time that the soul of your mother or father or some other person you loved had to spend in purgatory. For hundreds of years the Church had taught that Christians should pray for the souls of those who had died and ask God to be merciful to them; now people could do more than pray. They could buy an indulgence to ensure that the soul of the one they loved was let straight out of purgatory and into heaven. Many Catholic theologians and teachers before Luther were unhappy about the sale of these indulgences for the dead and had argued against it. But their protests had not had any effect. Simple people wanted to buy the indulgences to save their relatives and the Church desperately needed the money that the indulgences could raise. So the sale went on unchecked and rose to a crescendo in the early years of the sixteenth century.

The Jubilee Indulgence of 1513

In 1507 and again in 1513 the Pope declared a special Jubilee Indulgence to raise money to rebuild St Peter's in Rome. This 1513 indulgence, offered by Pope Leo X, could free both the living and the dead from their punishments in purgatory, even for the most 'grave and enormous' sins. Half the money from the sale of these indulgences in Germany was to go direct to the Pope for his building and his other expenses; the other half was also to be paid to the Pope to cancel the huge debt which the young Archbishop Albert of Mainz owed him. This Archbishop Albert – who was himself a prince and brother to the Elector of Brandenburg – owed the Pope thousands of ducats because the Pope had given him a special dispensation (in return for enormous fees) to hold three important bishoprics at once and to hold them all at the youthful age of twenty-four. As Archbishop of Mainz, he held the chief archbishopric in the whole of Germany. The wealthy banking house of Fugger handled the financial arrangements between Albert and the Pope and they took a share of the indulgence money for themselves.

Naturally, Archbishop Albert was anxious to sell as many indulgences as he could to clear his debts so he appointed a Dominican friar, John Tetzel, to go around the country preaching and persuading people to buy them. In their determination to sell a lot of indulgences, Tetzel and the other preachers went far beyond the proper teaching of the Church. The people who came to buy indulgences were led to believe that they were actually buying God's forgiveness for themselves or their dead relatives. This troubled Luther very much. He was sure that God's forgiveness was entirely free and could not be bought or sold. He did not like to see the Church getting rich by playing on people's fear of God's punishment. He did not want people to be misled into thinking that they could be saved – or their dead loved ones saved – by buying indulgences instead of simply by being sorry for their sins and having faith in God.

As Tetzel moved from town to town it was almost like a religious festival. This is how one eye-witness described it. 'The papal bull [the Pope's document proclaiming the Jubilee Indulgence] was carried on a satin or gold-embroidered cushion and all the priests and monks, the town council,

Johannes Tetzel von Leipzig

John Tetzel, in his Dominican habit, with a rack full of indulgences of different values, the papal authorization, and a money-box. This picture is by Brühl.

was probably printed late in 1521 or early 1522 at a time when Luther was mistakenly thought to be dead. It twice includes the famous jingle that Tetzel is said to have used:

As soon as the coin in the coffer rings
At once the soul up to heaven springs.

Whether Tetzel himself really used these words or whether they were attributed to him by his enemies, they do sum up his message. It was no wonder that the people who listened to Tetzel's preaching flocked around to pay their money and buy indulgences.

Luther's Ninety-five Theses

In 1517 Luther decided to protest about the sale of indulgences and the misleading preaching that went with them. He sent to Archbishop Albert a list of Ninety-five Theses or arguments against indulgences. He wrote a letter to Albert at the same time and said 'Simple folk . . . [believe] that when they have bought the indulgence they have secured their salvation. [They believe] that the moment the money jingles in the box, souls are delivered from purgatory and that all sins will be forgiven through a letter of indulgence. . . Ah, dear God! In this way the souls who are committed to your care, dear father, are being led in the paths of death. . . Christ has nowhere commanded indulgences to be preached, only the Gospel.'

Luther took another copy of his Ninety-five Theses and nailed them to the door of the Wittenberg church. This was the usual way for a professor to let people know that he was willing to have a public debate about some important issue. Luther was challenging other scholars to argue with him about the Ninety-five Theses, rather like a knight challenging all-comers to a joust.

These Ninety-five Theses, nailed up on 31 October 1517,

schoolmasters, scholars, men, women and children, all went out to meet Tetzel with banners and lighted tapers, with songs and processions. Then all the bells were rung and all the organs played.'

In the midst of all this enthusiasm, Tetzel would whip up the people with lurid descriptions of their loved ones burning in the fires of purgatory. The broadsheet shown on the next page

A cartoon by an unknown artist showing Tetzel selling indulgences and the people hurrying to buy them. Beside it is a full translation:

The title reads:

'John Tetzel, the Dominican monk, with his Roman indulgence-trash, which he put up for sale in Germany in the year of Christ 1517, as he is depicted in the church at Pirna in his homeland.'

The picture shows Tetzel as saying:

'O you Germans, mark me well. I am the servant of our Holy Father the Pope and am myself bringing to you 10,900 quarantines [=indulgences of 40 days]. Mercy and indulgence for sin for you, your parents, wife and child, shall be granted every one of you according to how much you put into the chest. As soon as the guilder rings in the plate, the soul in a jiffy leaps in [to] heaven.'

The satirical verses below the picture say:

'When Pope Leo, called the tenth, found it most unlikely that he would make it to the Jubilee Year [1525] he sent out the rotten wares of indulgence – trash for sale in Germany by his pedlars. Without demur John Tetzel let himself be used for this purpose. He had only just cheated the gallows, being about to be drowned for adultery, had not pious Prince Frederick taken up his cause and made most gracious intercession with the Emperor Maximilian. But things did not stop here and the adulterer became a thief, who by supposed power and might made a lot of money and property by persuading the blind world that he had heaven for sale: if you just produced enough money no one would be in any danger. As soon as the penny rings in the box the soul flies into heaven. With this devilish trumpery he deceived his homeland until God took a hand in his game through the late Doctor Luther, who violently overturned his pedlar's table. And so, God be praised, the indulgence-trash has lain scattered up to the present, and now the merits of Christ alone are all we gain. Tetzel's trash and the Pope's deceit have no title or currency with us.

¶ Amore et studio elucidande veritatis, hec subscripta disputabuntur Wittenburge Presidente R.P. Martino Luther Eremita no Augustiniano Artiũ et S. Theologie Magistro, eiusdemq̃ ibidem lectore Ordinario. Quare petit vt qui non possunt verbis presentes nobiscum disceptare / agant id literis absentes.
In Nomine dñi nostri Ihesu Christi. Amen.

1. Dñs et magister noster Ihesus Christus, dicendo penitẽtiã agite 2c. omnẽ vitam fidelium, penitentiam esse voluit.

2. Qd verbũ de penitẽtia sacrametali (i. cõfessionis et satisfactionis que sacer dotum ministerio celebratur) non potest intelligi.

3. Nõ tñ solã intẽdit interiorẽ: immo interior nulla est, nisi foris operetur varias carnis mortificationes.

4. Manet itacq̃ pena donec manet odiũ sui (i. penitẽtia vera intus) scz vsqz ad introitum regni celorum.

5. Papa nõ vult nec pot vllas penas remittere, preter eas, qs arbitrio vel suo vel canonum imposuit.

6. Papa nõ potest remittere vllã culpam, nisi declarando et approbando remissa a deo. Aut certe remittendo casus reservatos sibi, quibus contẽptis culpa prorsus remaneret.

7. Nulli prorsus remittit deus culpã, quin simul eũ subijciat humiliatũ in omnibus sacerdoti suo vicario.

8. Canones penitentiales solũ viuentibus sũt impositi, nihilcz morituris fm eosdem debet imponi.

9. Inde bñ nobis facit spũssanctus in papa, excipiendo in suis decretis semper articulum mortis et necessitatis.

38. Docendi sunt Christiani, qp Papa sicut magis eget ita magis optat: in venijs dandis p se deuotam orõnem, qp promptam pecuniam.

39. Docendi sunt Christiani, qp venie Pape sunt vtiles: si nõ in eas cõfidant: F nocentissime: si timorem dei per eas amittant.

40. Docendi sunt Christiani qp si Papa nosset exactiões venialiũ predicatorũ, mallet Basilica S. Petri in cineres ire, qp edificari cute carne 2 ossibus ouiũ suarũ.

41. Docendi sunt Christiani, qp Papa sicut debet ita vellet: etiã vẽdita (si opus sit) Basilica S. Petri, de suis pecunijs dare illis: a quorũ plurimis quida con donatores veniarum pecuniam eliciunt.

42. Vana est fiducia salutis p literas veniarũ etiã si Commissarius: immo Papa ipe suam animam p illis impignoraret.

43. Hostes Christi et Pape: sunt ij, qui propter venias predicãdas verbũ dei in alijs ecclesijs penitus silere iubent.

44. Iniuria fit vbo Dei: dũ in eodẽ fmõe: equale vel longius tps impenditur venijs qp illi.

45. Mens Pape necessario est qp si venie (qd minimũ est) vna cãpana: vnis põpis et ceremonijs celebrantur.

46. Euãgeliũ (qd maximũ est) centũ cãpanis: cẽtũ põpis: centũ ceremonijs predicetur.

above: Part of the first version of Luther's famous Theses, printed in 1517. The opening lines read as follows:

'Love for truth and the desire to bring it to light prompt a public discussion of the following propositions at Wittenberg under the chairmanship of the reverend father Martin Luther, Master of Arts and Sacred Theology and duly appointed professor on these subjects at that place. He requests that those who cannot be present to debate orally with us will do so by letter in their absence.
In the Name of Our Lord Jesus Christ. Amen.'

Here are some of the Theses:

1. When our Lord and Master Jesus Christ said, 'Repent' he wanted the entire life of believers to be one of penitence.

2. This word cannot be understood as referring to penance as a sacrament (that is, confession and satisfaction, as administered by the ministry of priests).

20. By full remission of all punishment, the Pope therefore does not actually mean 'all [punishment]' but only that which he imposed.

21. Therefore, those indulgence preachers err who say that man is by papal indulgence absolved from every punishment and saved . . .

27. They preach human doctrines who assert that as soon as the coin falls into the chest the soul flies upwards [out of purgatory] . . .

have become very famous. They provided the spark that set off the Reformation, although the causes of the Reformation were more complicated. The main point Luther was making in his Theses was that only God – not the Pope or priests – could forgive sins; that God's forgiveness was given freely to anyone who was sorry for his sins; and that God's forgiveness could not possibly be bought for money. Luther's Theses were written in plain strong Latin. His friends soon translated them into plain strong German and had hundreds of copies printed on the recently developed printing presses. Copies were sent all over Germany and sold in every market-place. Within a few weeks everyone who could read was reading them. Wherever they were read many people agreed with Luther. They were tired of paying out money for indulgences and they resented their German money being sent off to Rome to build the Pope's church. So instead of the academic debate in Wittenberg that Luther had expected, he soon found that the whole country was full of people talking and arguing about his Ninety-five Theses.

6 The conflict begins

Luther was astonished at the way people all over Germany and even beyond responded so enthusiastically to his Theses. He had no idea that the general feeling against indulgences was so strong. One important reason for this feeling was that the people who lived in the Holy Roman Empire were beginning to think of themselves as Germans – as men who belonged to a distinctive German nation with its own language and its own culture. They resented anyone from outside, any foreigner – even the Pope himself – drawing away their wealth or interfering in their lives. It was this resentment, this growing sense of *nationalism* that provided such fertile ground for Luther's ideas.

Yet without the invention of printing those ideas could never have spread like wildfire as they did. There had been many reformers before Luther but they were seldom known outside a small circle of supporters and many of them had been suppressed by the Church leaders. Luther's name and Luther's protests were known throughout the whole of Germany within a few weeks. If Luther's friends had had to copy out the Theses by hand the Reformation would never have got under way.

Three attempts to stop Luther: Heidelberg, Augsburg and Leipzig

Not surprisingly, the Church authorities in Rome began to be worried. They had heard reports from Archbishop Albert about Luther's views. Albert wanted Luther kept quiet and so in February 1518 Rome asked the Augustinian order to deal with him themselves. At about the same time the Dominicans, a rival order, began a campaign against Luther. You will remember that Tetzel was a Dominican. Tetzel himself and another Domincan called Wimpina drew up a list of their own theses against Luther's Ninety-five Theses and they made a formal charge of heresy against him at Rome. To charge

Dürer's picture, dated 1520, of a German printer screwing down his press. It was on presses like this that Luther's Ninety-five Theses and his pamphlets and manifestos and his German Bible were printed. Without them his ideas would not have spread as quickly and as far as they did.

someone with heresy was to say that his views were against the true Christian faith. The Dominicans hoped that Rome would declare Luther a heretic. The punishment for a heretic who refused to change his beliefs was being burned to death.

In April 1518, Luther walked all the way to Heidelberg for the chapter, or meeting, of his order and there he defended himself against those of his fellow-Augustinians who disagreed with his teaching. Many of the younger friars supported him and he emerged triumphant from the debates. 'I came by foot', he said, 'but I went home on a wagon.'

Once he was home in Wittenberg again he had to face the results of the Dominican charges against him. Frederick the Wise – the Elector of Saxony – had been ordered by Rome to give Luther up to be arrested by the Augustinians and to be taken to Rome to answer these charges. Frederick was most

Luther's interview in 1518 with Cajetan, who is seated at the table. The woodcut is from a German religious history printed in 1554.

unwilling to hand Luther over. He certainly did not agree with Luther's ideas but he was proud of his new university of Wittenberg and he did not want any interference from outside with this brilliant young professor. The Pope particularly wanted to avoid annoying Frederick – he needed his support in the anticipated election for a new Emperor. So it was agreed that instead of being taken off to Rome, Luther would be interviewed at Augsburg by Cardinal Cajetan, the Pope's representative, or 'legate', one of the Church's ablest theologians.

Again Luther travelled by foot and he arrived in Augsburg in October 1518 very weary and full of fear. He knew now that he was in real danger. He could be arrested and even put to death. His four interviews with Cajetan proved difficult. Cajetan demanded that Luther give up all his 'errors' and promise never to teach them again and never to cause any more trouble. Luther refused. Both men shouted angrily at each other and the final interview was suddenly broken off. Luther's friends were

afraid he might be arrested at any minute and so they smuggled him out of the city and took him back to Wittenberg.

The third challenge Luther had to meet was at Leipzig in June and July of the following year, 1519. Here his opponent was Doctor John Eck. The first day of the disputation, as it was called, began with a special mass very early in the morning, then a splendid procession; then speeches of welcome. Then musicians played and a choir sang a new hymn to the Holy Spirit. Finally everyone went to lunch. Only after lunch did the trumpets sound and the business really begin. The hall of the castle was packed full. Many of Luther's students had come with him from Wittenberg to hear the debate. One man who was present, Peter Mosellanus, wrote to a friend to tell him all about it. This is how he described the two opponents – you will see that he was not unbiased! 'Martin is of middle height with a slender body worn out both by study and care, so that you can almost count his bones. He is in the vigour of manhood; his voice is sharp and clear. . . He is vivacious and sure, always

25

Luther's meeting with Doctor John Eck at Leipzig in 1519; another woodcut from the 1554 history. Eck was to appear again eleven years later at the Diet of Augsburg when he put the Catholic case against the Augsburg Confession (see p. 46).

with a happy face no matter how hard his enemies press him. . . Eck has a tall stature, a solid, square body, a full German voice, strong lungs as of an actor or town-crier, but giving out a rough rather than a clear sound. . . His mouth and eyes, or rather his whole face, would make you think him a butcher or a soldier rather than a theologian.'

Eck pressed Luther hard and taunted him with supporting the views of the notorious Bohemian heretic, John Huss, who had been burned for his teachings a hundred years earlier. Luther shocked the crowd by declaring that many of Huss's views were truly Christian and that the church council that had condemned

Huss might have made a mistake. This suggestion was quite unthinkable to Luther's opponents. For the first time Luther began to realize that he was not just involved in a debate about indulgences. He was, as his opponents said, challenging the power of the Pope and the authority of the Church itself. Over the next few months he had to think out more fully what he wanted to say. It was a turning point in his life. 'Farewell, unhappy, hopeless, blasphemous Rome!' he wrote. 'Let us leave her then that she may become the dwelling-place of dragons, spectres and witches!'

7 The three manifestos of 1520

In 1520 Luther wrote three pamphlets or manifestos. These are among the most important documents of the Reformation. Like the Ninety-five Theses they were quickly printed and sent throughout Germany. Everyone was discussing them. The Pope's legate in Germany wrote home to Rome in great alarm: 'By now the whole of Germany is in full revolt; nine-tenths raise the war-cry "Luther" while the watchword of the other tenth, who are indifferent to Luther, is "Death to the Roman Curia".' Pictures of Luther, some even with a halo round his head like pictures of the saints, were sold in the market-places. He was becoming a national hero. What did Luther say in these three manifestos which really set the Reformation on its way? In all three he was protesting against things that he thought were wrong in the Church and setting out the reforms he hoped to see.

'To the Christian Nobility of the German Nation' is the shortened title of the first manifesto and it began: 'The time for silence is gone and the time to speak has come.'

This is the earliest portrait we have of Martin Luther. It appeared on the title-page of a sermon he preached which was published in Leipzig in 1519. The words were cut the wrong way round, perhaps because the pamphlet was being rushed to the printer.

far right: The title page of one of Luther's three manifestos of 1520. This one is called *To the Christian Nobility of the German Nation.* The picture shows you the way a noble or knight would have dressed in Luther's time, but, to judge by the way the sword is being worn, this also has been printed in reverse.

The title page of Luther's second great manifesto 'On the Babylonish Captivity of the Church' in which he argued that the Church was enslaved by sacramental rules and that there should be only three sacraments: 'baptism, penance and the bread'. He wanted lay people as well as clergy to be able to drink from the cup at communion.

tivity of the Church' and was mainly about the sacraments. Luther felt that the Church was enslaved by the complicated system of sacramental rules and practices and by the clergy who administered them. He likened this to the time the Israelites spent in exile as captives in Babylon. The Church taught that there were seven sacraments: baptism, holy communion, penance, confirmation, ordination, matrimony and extreme unction. Luther wrote, 'I must deny that there are seven sacraments and must lay it down for the time being that there are only three, baptism, penance and the bread.' By 'the bread' Luther meant the holy communion, or the Lord's Supper as the reformers came to call it. Later Luther decided that penance, though a valuable practice, was not really a sacrament. He insisted that there were just two sacraments commanded by Jesus – 'baptism and the bread'. Baptism was always very important to Luther. Whenever he was in despair about himself and his failings, he would hold on to the simple fact, 'I am baptised'. To him baptism was a sign that God would always go on forgiving him. 'Baptism means two things', he wrote, 'death and resurrection; that is full and complete justification. When the minister dips the child into the water, this means death; when he draws him out again, this means life.'

Justification by faith

In his third manifesto, 'Concerning Christian Liberty', Luther set out again the discovery he had made in his reading of Romans. Christians, he said, were freely given God's goodness when they had faith in Jesus Christ. They were justified by faith alone. This cry of *sola fide*, by faith alone, is one of the keys to Luther's thought and to the revolution he led against the vast organization of the Catholic Church. He believed that the Church, which wielded such immense power over the

Luther was writing here to the nobles – a particularly influential class in Germany. If he could win *their* support, his reforms would stand a much better chance of success. He argued in this manifesto that all Christians were equal and that bishops, priests and monks were not – as was generally thought – of a higher or more spiritual state than other people. He said that the Pope did not have the right to decide what the Bible meant. He believed that this was the right of the whole Christian community. He said that priests should be allowed to marry. He wanted the universities to be reformed so that, in place of Aristotle's philosophy, students could learn the Biblical languages – Greek and Hebrew – and mathematics and history. He wanted boys taught the Bible in school and he added: 'Would to God each town had also a girls' school in which girls might be taught the Gospel for an hour daily, either in German or Latin.' 'A spinner or a seamstress teaches her daughter her trade while she is young', he wrote, 'but now even the most learned bishops and prelates do not know the Gospel.'

The second manifesto was called 'On the Babylonish Cap-

The title page of the Pope's bull 'Against the errors of Martin Luther and his followers'. Besides the papal insignia, it carries Pope Leo's family arms, the Medici 'pills', with the lilies of Florence, and has typical Italian Renaissance decoration round the border.

whole western world, had imprisoned the gospel of God's forgiveness in a rigid system of laws and rules and power politics. He wanted to go back to what he was sure was the simple message of hope in the New Testament – that people do not have to 'earn' their salvation by doing good deeds ('good works') or by fasting or keeping rules. He insisted that Christians would in fact do good and loving deeds, not to earn God's approval but simply in gratitude for God's forgiveness. Faith came first, then God's free forgiveness, then 'good works' naturally followed. 'From faith flow forth love and joy in the Lord', he wrote, 'and from love a cheerful, willing, free spirit, ready to serve our neighbour freely. . . I will give myself as a Christ to my neighbour just as Christ offered himself to me.'

The people who read Luther's teaching in these three manifestos about the equality of all Christian believers, about the sacraments and about justification by faith, felt they had been set free. However burdened with restrictions and anxiety the Lutheran and Reformed Churches later became, at least at its beginning the Reformation had this exciting quality of freedom.

The papal bull 'Exsurge Domine'

In May 1520, a bull (that is a proclamation by the Pope) was issued from Rome to condemn Luther. This bull is known as *Exsurge Domine* because these are its opening words in Latin. Translated into English, the bull begins, 'Arise O Lord. . . A wild boar is seeking to destroy thy vineyard.' The bull said that Luther had sixty days in which to give up all his errors or he would be declared a heretic and excommunicated – that is cut off from the sacraments of the Church. Luther's response was 'I will do what I believe to be right.' He realized that the time had come when he could no longer obey the Pope. He saw the Pope now not as the representative of Christ on earth but as the

Bulla contra errores Martini Lutheri z sequacium.

A woodcut of 1554 showing Luther burning the books of the canon law — all the rules of the Church. Historians think that perhaps it was Luther's followers who put these books on the fire, but it seems likely that he himself threw on the Pope's bull that had condemned him and his teachings.

The title page of a sermon preached at St Paul's, London, by Bishop John Fisher of Rochester. This sermon was an attack on Luther and was preached on the occasion of the public burning of Luther's writings. It was printed in Cambridge in 1521 by John Siberch.

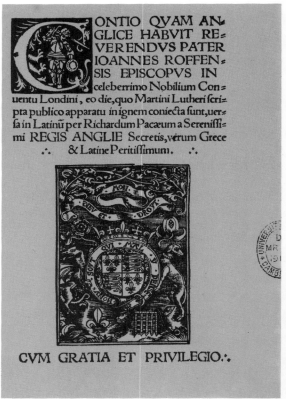

'deadly enemy of Christ'. On 10 December 1520, Luther gave a vivid public demonstration of his beliefs. His friend Agricola lit a huge bonfire near the gate of Wittenberg. Crowds of students, lecturers, townspeople and monks gathered round. Into the flames were thrown the books of the canon law. These were the books that set out all the rules, laws and practices of the Church. Then in went books about penance which, Luther believed, had entangled men's minds in fear. Finally, Luther himself stepped forward and threw in the papal bull, *Exsurge Domine*. It flared up and burned away to ashes in the bonfire. Luther was openly defying the Pope. His gesture was like a declaration of war.

8 The Diet of Worms, April 1521

The climax of these three years of conflict between Martin Luther and the Church came at the Diet of Worms in April 1521. The new Emperor, Charles V, was preparing to hold his first 'parliament' (called the Diet) at the old town of Worms. The Pope had already condemned Luther, not only in the bull *Exsurge Domine* but a second time by a complete and final excommunication in the bull *Decet Romanum* of January 1521. The Pope's new legate in Germany, Jerome Aleander, was anxious that Charles and his Diet should add their condemnation to the Pope's. He wanted to be sure that Luther was outlawed by the State as well as by the Church. The Emperor Charles had no sympathy with Luther, but he promised Luther's prince, Frederick the Wise, that he would let him travel in safety to and from the Diet at Worms. Luther, in his turn, had been approached by Ulrich von Hutten, a knight who was also a famous scholar. Von Hutten believed that the best thing for Germany would be an armed rising by the knights who would destroy the prince-bishops. He even hoped that he and Luther might work together, and indeed pictures of them side by side were being sold. But Luther did not want war and he said 'No' to von Hutten. 'I refuse to fight for the Gospel with force and slaughter', he wrote. 'If the Gospel were something that could have been saved by war, God would surely never have entrusted it to fishermen.'

So on 16 April Luther came to Worms to face the Emperor and his Diet. Von Hutten and his knights were waiting nearby, all ready with their weapons and their armour in the Ebernburg castle hoping to launch a war if they saw the chance. The crowds began to fill the streets of Worms long before Luther arrived. When at last he appeared, still dressed in his black monk's habit and riding in a horse-drawn cart, the crowd shouted and cheered in welcome.

The next afternoon Luther came before the Diet. He was shown an enormous pile of all the books he had ever written.

Copper engraving of Ulrich von Hutten, a leader of the knights who wanted Luther's support in an armed revolt. Von Hutten's crown symbolizes his fame as a Renaissance scholar and humanist.

The handwritten notes that Luther made the night before his speech at the Diet of Worms.

An official spoke for the Emperor and asked Luther two questions: 'Did you write all these books?' and 'Will you now take back the things you said in these books?' All the titles of the books were read out one by one. Luther agreed that he had written them all. Then he asked for time to consider the second question. He was told sharply that he did not deserve any longer time but the Emperor agreed to give him one day to think over his answer.

That night Luther made a few notes on a piece of paper. We still have that piece of paper today and can see what he hoped to say. The next day, 18 April, Luther arrived at the Diet at four o'clock. Such an enormous crowd had packed into the hall, together with the members of the Diet itself, that the whole proceedings had to be moved to a larger hall. By the time Luther's turn came it was getting dark and torches had to be lit around the crowded room. Again Luther was asked if he would take back and deny the things he had written in his books. Luther then made his speech. He said he had written two kinds of books. Some were devotional books about the Gospel and no one objected to those. Others were books attacking things he thought were wrong in the Church. He went on to defend these books but he was interrupted by an official who said, 'I insist that you give your answer. Will you or will you not revoke your books and their errors?'

Then Luther gave his answer, speaking first in Latin and then in German. 'Unless I am convinced, by scripture or by plain reason. . . I cannot and I will not recant. . . It is neither safe nor right to go against one's conscience. God help me. Amen.'

The crowd broke out into a confusion of shouting, cheering and protesting. Luther was hurried out of the hall. A few days later he was at last given the chance to argue his case with a bishop and two skilled laymen but this debate fell rather flat and no agreement could be reached. Finally the Emperor proclaimed his edict against Luther. Luther was now to be an outlaw of the Holy Roman Empire as well as excommunicated by the Church. The edict said to all the people of the Empire: 'You shall refuse the aforesaid Martin Luther hospitality, lodging and bed; none shall feed and nourish him with food or drink;. . . wherever you meet him . . . you shall take him prisoner and deliver him to us. . . As for his friends . . . and supporters . . . we order that you shall attack, overthrow, seize and wrest their property from them, taking it all into your own possession. . . As for the books of Martin Luther . . . we order that nobody shall dare to buy, sell, keep, copy, print them . . . or support, preach, defend or assert them in any way. . . We decree . . . that the works of Luther are to be burned and by this and other means utterly destroyed.'

The Pope, in his bull of excommunication, had used similar words. Martin Luther and his followers were to be 'excommunicated, accursed, condemned, heretics, hardened, . . . deprived of possessions. . . The faithful Christians, one and all, shall be told strictly to shun these men.'

This double condemnation by Church and State hung over Luther for the rest of his life. At any time he could have been arrested and imprisoned. All of his books and furniture could have been destroyed. But in fact he went free. He stayed always within Saxony where the support of the people and the protection of the Elector made sure that the Emperor's edict could never be carried out.

right: Luther at the Diet of Worms; another picture from the 1554 history. Luther is in front on the extreme left looking across to the Emperor. Next to him is his lawyer, Dr Jerome Schurpff who was Professor of Law in the university of Wittenberg. Schurpff is calling out the Latin words that have been written next to him: 'Intitulentur libri' (Let the titles be read!) He insisted that the titles of all the books must be read out aloud before Luther could admit to having written them. The German words at the very bottom of the picture mean: 'Here I stand. I cannot do otherwise. God help me. Amen.' For hundreds of years it has been believed that Luther said these very words but the earliest accounts of the Diet do not mention them at all. Even if the words are a legend, they do suggest something of Luther's spirit and of the way he was feeling as he faced the Emperor and princes.

The 'capture' of Luther

Luther, still protected by the safe-conduct, had left Worms for Wittenberg some weeks before the imperial ban was proclaimed. Frederick the Wise wanted to shield him if he could, but without openly defying the ban, so a plan was made between Frederick and Luther's friends to 'kidnap' him on his way home to Wittenberg and to keep him safely in hiding till the immediate danger died down. The plan worked well. As Luther travelled through the dark forest near Eisenach, riding in a cart, he was suddenly ambushed by a troop of horsemen. He was bundled on to a horse and carried off to the Wartburg castle. Here he was safe as the 'prisoner' of Frederick. Rumours flew around the countryside that he was arrested by the Emperor and even that he was dead. He wrote to his good friend, George Spalatin, secretary to Frederick: 'I was stripped of my own clothes and dressed in those of a knight. I am letting my hair and my beard grow and you would hardly know me – indeed for some time I haven't recognized myself! I am now living in Christian freedom. . . Farewell, and pray for me.'

right: Martin Luther disguised as Junker George, a country gentleman; painted by Cranach the elder.

9 'Prisoner' in the Wartburg

The Wartburg as it is today, massive on its dominating height surrounded by forests. Here Luther was kept safe from April 1521 until early in 1522, and here he translated the New Testament into German.

After the first excitement of the 'capture' had died down, Luther was faced with a long and very lonely time in the Wartburg. He was often ill, he slept badly, and he was sometimes overcome by despair and temptation. He wrote to his friend, Philip Melanchthon, 'I *should* be afire in the spirit; in reality I am afire in the flesh, with lust, laziness, idleness, sleepiness . . . . Pray for me, I beg you, for in my seclusion here I am submerged in sin.'

Sometimes Luther managed to get away from the Wartburg for a few hours to ride into the surrounding countryside. He was disguised by his long hair and beard and his knight's clothes. The local people called him 'Junker George'. Once, in 1521, he even went as far as Wittenberg on a secret visit. While he was there, Lucas Cranach the elder made a picture of him, so we have a good idea of what he looked like disguised as 'Junker George'. (The picture is on page 33.)

One man who chanced to meet 'Junker George' was John Kessler, a student from Switzerland. Many years later he wrote an account of this meeting for his small sons. Kessler was on his way to Wittenberg with a fellow-student. Night fell when they were in the countryside near the Wartburg, and they tried to find somewhere to stay but all the inns were full. At last the landlord of the Black Bear agreed to take them in. They clumped into the parlour in their muddy boots, and there saw a man, sitting alone and reading a book while he ate his dinner. He was dressed as a knight in 'red hood, plain doublet and hose, a sword at his side, his right hand on its hilt and the other on the book'. This man asked the students to join him at his meal. They did so and told him they were going to Wittenberg, hoping to hear the great Martin Luther. But the man told them that Luther was definitely not there. He urged them to study Hebrew and Greek so they could understand the Bible better and to hear Philip Melanchthon's lectures. Kessler and his friend thought that this man was a most unusual knight!

Luther's study in the Wartburg.

Then the landlord took Kessler aside and told him that the knight was really Martin Luther himself. Kessler hurried back to his friend and whispered, 'Don't look now, but that man is Martin Luther!' The students were overcome with awe, but Luther talked with them for hours and even paid their bill at the end of the evening.

Translating the Bible

While Luther was in the Wartburg, he began and finished one of the most important things he ever did. He translated the whole of the New Testament from Greek — the language in which it was first written — into the everyday German spoken by the people. 'This book', Luther wrote to George Spalatin, 'is to be written in the simplest language so that all may understand it.' At the same time he was writing pamphlets against the Pope. He increasingly used the rude and abusive language about his enemies that people used then in quarrels about religions. He called the Pope's supporters 'papist back-biters' and 'papal asses, mad and foolish'. He called the Pope himself 'Satan' and 'the Devil' and the 'Prince of Hell'. Meanwhile Luther's enemies were busy writing pamphlets attacking *him*, and they used similar violent and crude words. This pamphlet war raged on for years, always a strange mixture of reasonable arguments and violent insults.

While he was in the Wartburg, Luther also began work on translating the Old Testament from Hebrew into German. This took him much longer, and it was not finished for many years. He particularly loved the book of the Psalms. 'Would you like', he wrote, 'to see the holy Christian Church painted in living colour and form and put into one little picture? Then take up the Psalter [the book of Psalms] and you have a fine, bright, pure mirror that will show you what the Church is; and, you will find yourself also in it and the true *know thyself*, and

God himself besides, and all creatures.' Monks and priests had always said the Psalms in Latin in their prayers every day but now ordinary people could read them every day in German. Luther was later to use them as the basis for many of the hymns he wrote for people to sing in church and at home. In every country to which the Reformation spread, the Psalms were said or sung by the people in their own language, both in public worship and in private prayer. The Psalter was the chief prayer-book and hymn-book of the Reformation.

As Luther loved the Psalms in the Old Testament, so in the New Testament he loved St John's Gospel far more than

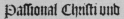

△ Two pictures from a very popular series of 1521 showing the contrast between Christ and Antichrist. On the left, Christ is seen humbly accepting the crown of thorns that is cruelly forced onto his head; on the right the Pope is shown seated in splendour and receiving an Emperor's crown.

Illustrations from Luther's Bible of 1534. The first shows Elijah being taken up into heaven in the fiery chariot (II Kings 2: 1–15). The second is at the beginning of St John's Gospel and it shows St John with his emblem, the eagle. He is looking towards the risen Christ. The third picture shows the Whore of Babylon riding on the seven-headed monster and wearing the papal crown. Luther took Revelation 17: 3–6 to be a foretelling of the Pope's power, but Luther's opponents saw *him* as a seven-headed monster (see p.5).

Matthew, Mark or Luke. He said it was the 'one, tender, true, chief Gospel'. His other great love was for Paul's Letter to the Romans which he called 'the very purest Gospel . . . a bright light, almost enough to light up all the scriptures'. He thought that everyone should know it by heart. Romans was to Luther the 'daily bread of the soul'.

This cartoon gives a good idea of the feelings that were set off by Luther. Not only is the Pope shown as Antichrist, but also as Leo, the lion, the king of the beasts. So his followers also become beasts, with the aid of some puns on their names.

A woodcut by Erhard Schoen showing iconoclasts – people who destroyed holy pictures and statues in churches. Some of Luther's followers behaved like this but Luther himself tried to stop them. The group of figures in the top right hand corner of the picture illustrate the parable of the mote and the beam (Luke 6:41–2).

Karlstadt's reforms in Wittenberg

Luther worked in the Wartburg on his translation of the Bible and back in Wittenberg most people thought he was dead or at least imprisoned by his enemies. Albrecht Dürer the artist, who lived in Nuremberg, wrote, 'O God, if Luther be dead, who will proclaim the Gospel so clearly to us?' There was a sudden upsurge of reforms in Wittenberg and at its centre was one of Luther's colleagues, Andrew Karlstadt. Monks were leaving their monasteries to get married; people were being given the cup as well as the bread at communion; priests were no longer wearing the richly embroidered vestments in church; some people were eating meat on fast-days. Luther was in two minds about all these changes when he heard of them. He approved of most of them but he felt that Wittenberg was rushing into too many reforms too quickly. He knew it took people a long while to get used to change in the Church.

Perhaps he was rather annoyed that the reforms were going ahead without him! Then news came that mobs of people were bursting into the churches and breaking up pictures and statues of the saints. Luther was alarmed that full revolution might break out and early in 1522 he put on his black habit again and hurried back to Wittenberg. He preached eight sermons in the church against the violence and destruction. Those who had thought he was dead were astonished to see him alive and well. He tried to persuade everyone to stop breaking images and to go on with Church reform at a gentler pace. He was sure that the first thing was to 'win the heart' by telling people about Jesus Christ. Then the images would become harmless and useless.

Now that he was back in Wittenberg, Luther realized that he had become tired of his isolation in the Wartburg so he decided to stay in Wittenberg and not worry any more about the danger of arrest.

10 Reforming the Church

Luther believed that reform should be allowed to come gently and always without force. 'I opposed indulgences and all the papists but never with force. I simply taught, preached and wrote God's Word; otherwise I did nothing. And while I slept or drank Wittenberg beer with my friends Philip and Amsdorf, the Word of God so greatly weakened the papacy that no prince or emperor ever inflicted such losses upon it. I did nothing. The Word did everything.'

Gradually the reforms that Luther hoped to see were brought in not just in Wittenberg but in towns and villages all over Germany. How was the new Church different from the old Catholic Church? What were the changes that everyone would notice?

Ministers

In the churches that had been reformed there were no priests – or rather, *everyone* was a priest. This is called the 'priesthood of all believers' and means that all Christians are equal before God and all can approach Him directly. Worship was not to be led by a priest as in the old Church but by a minister or pastor. Luther wanted the minister to be chosen by the people of the parish, not chosen by a bishop as before. In practice it was often the local town council who chose on behalf of the people. The minister was generally married and was given a house and a salary. Many of the ministers were former priests; others were former merchants, printers, schoolteachers. Some of them, especially in the villages, were quite untrained and Luther had to write books of sermons for them as they could not make up their own. These books, called Postils, were reprinted again and again and were widely used in Germany. Just as the ministers were to be equal with all the people and not a higher 'caste', so all ministers were to be equal with each other. There were no bishops, no monks, no Pope (though

later some Lutheran churches did re-introduce bishops). The only head of the church was Christ.

Worship and hymns

When the people came to church on Sundays they would be struck by a great change. The minister was now presiding at a meal, not offering a sacrifice. He spoke and the people replied in German, not in Latin. He wore a plain black robe, not

Martin Luther preaching at Wittenberg. This picture by Lucas Cranach (probably mainly by the Younger) is part of the altarpiece in the Wittenberg town church. In the full picture Luther is pointing at the figure of Christ on the cross and the people are listening to him and looking at Christ.

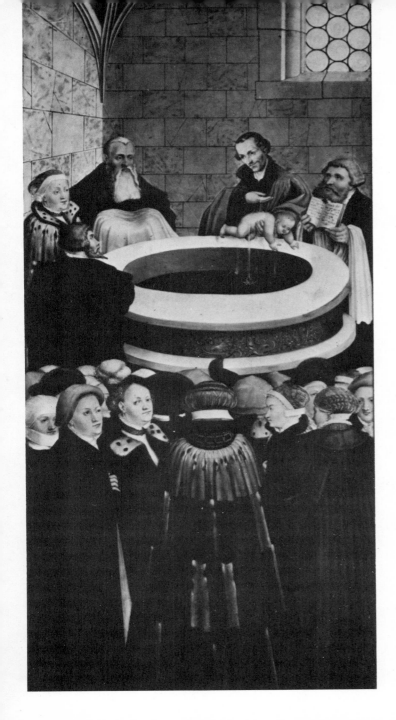

Another picture from the altarpiece in Wittenberg by Lucas Cranach (probably the Younger). It shows Luther's friend, Philip Melanchthon, baptizing a baby in the font.

coloured vestments. The sermon, when the minister explained the Bible to the people, became longer and more important. At communion the people were given the cup to drink from, as well as the consecrated bread to eat. They took the bread and the cup into their own hands. There were to be no more 'private masses' to be said for the repose of the souls of the dead – a minister was not to conduct worship without a congregation.

Perhaps the most startling change of all was the singing. In the old Church it was the choir that did almost all of the singing; the people just listened. The music sung by the choir was plainsong – a very beautiful and solemn kind of music. Luther wanted the people themselves to sing praise to God. He knew that they were fond of singing their own carols and folk-songs in their homes and out in the fields. Luther liked singing them himself. So he made up some hymns, sometimes using the folk tunes that people knew already and sometimes composing new tunes or getting better musicians than himself to compose them. These tunes made frequent use of repetition and often had a strong syncopated rhythm. This made them easy to learn. Luther made up the words of the hymns too and soon other writers were making up more. Some of his hymns are based on the Psalms; some are translations of the old Latin hymns; some are about the teachings of Jesus; some are about the central beliefs of the Church like the resurrection. Soon these hymns became wildly popular throughout Germany and beyond. People were singing them not just in church but at home and at work on the farms. The hymns became one of the chief ways of teaching people about the Christian faith, just as in the old Church the statues and stained-glass windows were used to teach people. The Lutheran Church was always a singing Church. It never had that suspicion of music that some later reformed churches had. This Lutheran musical tradition was

A fort-ress sure___ is God our King, A shield that ne'er shall fail___ us; His sword a - lone___ shall suc-cour bring, When e - vil doth as-sail___ us, With craft___ and cru - el hate, Doth Satan lie in wait, And armed with dead-ly power, Seeks whom he may de - vour, On earth where is his___ e - qual.

greatly enriched two hundred years later by the music of J. S. Bach.

Some of Luther's hymns are still sung today. One of the best known is 'Ein' feste Burg ist unser Gott'. The tune as you will find it in most hymn books is not exactly as Luther wrote it. Here is something much nearer to Luther's original melody. If you would like to sing the words to this older version of the tune you will have to put in an extra note as shown at the points marked ★. This hymn became the 'battle hymn' of the Reformation and was sung defiantly by Protestants all over Europe as a sign of their break from Rome. Today, fortunately, it is no longer a battle hymn and is sung by Catholics as well as by Protestants.

The Bible

The German Bible, in Luther's translation, with woodcuts by Cranach and other artists, was printed and sold throughout the country. Many families could now have their own copy of the Bible and could read it at home as well as hearing it in church. Home-centred, family-centred religion became more and more important. The Bible itself, whether read in private or preached in church moved to the centre of people's Christian lives and, in a sense, took the place that the seven sacraments had held in the Catholic Church.

The Catechisms

Luther wrote two catechisms – the Large and the Small. A catechism is a book that sets out clearly, in questions and answers, the meaning of Christian beliefs. When Luther travelled around the villages he was appalled to find that often the people knew nothing about the Christian faith. 'Merciful God! What misery I have seen!' he wrote. 'The common people . . . know neither the Lord's Prayer nor the Creed nor the Ten Commandments, but live like the poor cattle and the

This woodcut by Cranach shows, on the left, the Lutheran view of the two sacraments and of the preaching of the Word. On the right is the Lutheran view of how sacraments and preaching were abused in the Catholic Church.

senseless swine.' His Small Catechism was plain and simple. It explained the meaning of the Ten Commandments and the Apostles' Creed (which had always been taught by the Catholic Church and continued to be taught by both the Catholic and Protestant Churches after the Reformation). It taught the Lord's Prayer and finally the meaning of the two sacraments – baptism and the Lord's Supper. This catechism was used for teaching children and adults in church and at home as well as in school. Luther's wife Katherine was one of the many people who were helped by this little catechism. 'This book tells all about me', she said.

The schools

Now that the Bible was so much more important it also became important that people could read it. There was a great need for more schools so that people could learn to read. Luther encouraged the towns to set up schools for boys and girls and also classes in the evening for adults. At the new Wittenberg boys' school, founded in 1533, the pupils sat on wooden benches. All the classes were in the one big room with the youngest near the front. School began at 5.30 a.m. in summer and 6.30 a.m. in winter. All the teaching was still in Latin though the catechism was learned in German as well as Latin. At the Wittenberg girls' school the girls learned reading, writing, music, mathematics, the Bible and the catechism. Luther said that the girls should be punished less severely than the boys when they did not learn their lessons! This network of new schools throughout Germany helped to spread the Reformation.

A woodcut of 1522 showing a triple wedding ceremony. In front a bishop is being married, behind and to the right a monk; and at the left a friar is being married to a nun. Two musicians are playing cheerfully in the background.

The closing of the monasteries

Many monks and nuns left their monasteries and convents at the time of the Reformation because they no longer believed it was the best way of living a Christian life. Others were forced to leave, against their will, by violent mobs of people. These same mobs often looted the monastery buildings, destroying images and carrying off priceless treasures and books. Although Luther himself was strongly opposed to this destruction and violence, it still went on in many parts of the country and caused much suffering and bitterness.

Most of the monks who left got married and took up ordinary life in the world. Some became ministers (or pastors); others became influential leaders in the towns. The wealth and lands of the monasteries sometimes passed into the hands of local nobles and sometimes they were taken over by the towns. Luther wanted the towns to put this money from the monasteries into a 'common chest' to pay for schools and the minis-ter's salary and to help the sick and poor. These were all jobs that the monasteries had often done before the Reformation and now the towns had to take them on. The closing of the monasteries, then, brought many social changes in Germany, particularly in the provision of education and in caring for the poor and the sick.

The Peasants' War

From 1518 onwards, Luther had found great support and sympathy amongst the poor peasants, who were by far the largest class in Germany. They had heard his message as one of freedom from every kind of oppression – oppression by their landlords as well as oppression by the clergy. In this they were encouraged by agitators who wanted to use Luther's ideas for political ends. Luther himself sympathized with the peasants and was openly critical of the wealthy rulers and landlords who often exploited them.

Peasants overrun and plunder a monastery in the uprisings of 1525. The drawing comes from a manuscript account of the Peasants' War.

Towards the end of 1524, the peasants' demands for cheaper food and greater freedom became more insistent. A series of violent risings broke out and gathered force in many parts of the country. Thousands of peasants armed themselves as best they could and made open attacks on monasteries, castles and prosperous farms. They surged through the countryside, living off the land, and killing, burning, plundering as they went. These violent risings, known as the Peasants' War, were soon severely put down by the rulers' armies who were far stronger than the poorly equipped, disorganized peasants.

The peasants were disillusioned when they did not get from Luther any of the support they had expected. Quite the opposite. He was so horrified at the prospect of a bloody revolution that he urged the rulers to crush the rebels without mercy. 'Let everyone who can', he wrote to the ruling princes in his pamphlet *Against the Robbing and Murdering Hordes of Peasants*, May 1525, 'smite, slay and stab, secretly or openly, remembering that nothing can be more poisonous, hurtful or devilish than a rebel. It is just as when one must kill a mad dog; if you do not strike him, he will strike you, and a whole land with you.' Luther believed that Christians ought always to obey their rulers – even unjust rulers – and that rebellion against the state was always wrong and must be crushed. This ruthless attitude of Luther's towards the rebel peasants in 1525 shocked many of his supporters at the time and has gone on troubling people ever since.

43

11 Luther and his family

Luther's marriage

When Luther had heard, back in the Wartburg, that monks were getting married he said, 'Good heavens! They won't give *me* a wife!' But he changed his mind. In 1523 he helped a group of nine nuns to leave their convent and come to Wittenberg. Two years later all of them had found husbands except one, Katherine von Bora. Luther suggested someone she might marry but she refused. Then Luther, with her consent, married her himself. It was June 1525. He was forty-two and she was twenty-six. This was the unromantic and commonsense beginning of what turned out to be a very happy marriage. Luther's father came to the wedding party and at last forgave his son for going into a monastery in the first place and then for leaving it.

'Before I was married', said Luther, 'my bed was not made for a whole year and it was rotting with my sweat.' He certainly needed looking after. But he did not find the first year of marriage easy. He would wake up in the night and see with surprise Katherine's pigtails on the pillow beside him. She talked a lot and he found that rather wearing!

Martin Luther and his wife Katherine, painted by Cranach at the time of their marriage in June 1525.

Luther with his friends and family at the meal table. The jottings which the students made through the meal were later published as Luther's *Table Talk*, and this picture comes from the 1568 edition.

Martin and Katherine lived in part of the Augustinian monastery at Wittenberg where Luther had been a friar. They had five children of their own – a sixth died very young and one of the five, Magdalena, died when she was fifteen. They also brought up eleven orphan nephews and nieces. In addition to all these children there were always about twelve student-lodgers and an endless stream of visitors. The house was so full of people and noise and so chaotic with papers, books and children's toys that one prince was warned by his friends not to stay there if he wanted to get a good night's sleep!

Katherine was a very capable manager. She not only looked after this enormous household (which meant getting up at four in the morning), but she grew vegetables in the garden, kept pigs, cows and goats, and brewed beer. At meal times she used to get very annoyed with the students who sat each with his notebook beside his soup-plate, carefully jotting down every word Luther spoke. She was sharp with Luther too when he talked on and on through the meal. 'Why don't you eat instead of always talking?' she would say. She pulled him up firmly when his language became too rough – as it often did.

Luther was not easy to live with. He was often moody and depressed and at other times gay and energetic. He was frequently ill. Katherine found him a difficult patient to look after. She was a great believer in the popular and unpleasant cures of the day – giving the patient cow's dung or pig's dung in wine, for example! Luther hated these remedies but he had to put up with them.

Although there were difficult times in the Luther family, there were also very happy times. Luther loved music and often played the lute and sang with his children and all the other people in his house. He liked pottering in his garden and he enjoyed eating well and drinking good wine and beer. He worked with tremendous energy and concentration and kept up a steady flow of pamphlets, books, Biblical commentaries and lectures all through his life. When he had to travel away from home he missed Katie (as he called Katherine) and the children very much and wrote them warm and amusing letters. He teased Katie in his letters because she was always worrying about him. 'To the saintly anxious lady, Katherine Luther . . . my gracious dear wife', he wrote, 'Grace and peace in Christ. Most saintly lady doctoress, we thank you kindly for your great care for us, which stopped you sleeping, for since you began to be so anxious we were nearly consumed by a fire in our inn . . . and yesterday . . . a stone fell upon our heads and almost crushed us as in a mousetrap. . . If you do not stop worrying the earth may at last swallow us up. . . Pray, and leave it to God to care for us.'

12 From Luther to Lutheranism

In the years that had passed since Luther faced the Emperor Charles at the Diet of Worms in 1521, Charles had been kept very busy outside Germany with difficult though successful wars in Italy against the King of France. He heard alarming reports of the spread of Luther's ideas and he decided at the first opportunity to settle the problem once and for all. He called a meeting of the Diet for April 1530 in Augsburg. The Catholics were hoping he would crush the Protestants, as the reformers were now called. (They had been given this name at the Diet of Speyer in 1529 when the Lutheran princes had *protested* against the decision of the Catholic majority not to allow them each to be responsible for the religious faith in his own state.) The Protestants in their turn were hoping to be given complete freedom to worship in their own way. They wanted to explain to Charles that they did not intend to split the Church but that they were asking for freedom *within* the Church to go back to the beliefs and practices of the early Church as seen in the New Testament.

The Elector of Saxony – now John who had succeeded Frederick the Wise – came to Augsburg with the delegation of reformers. Luther was one of them but he had to be left in Coburg castle – much to his disappointment! As he was still an outlaw of the Empire, it would not have been safe for him to enter Augsburg. His gentle friend, Philip Melanchthon, had to present the Protestant case instead of Luther. He drew up a document that set out all the points of the Christian faith on which all the Protestant groups agreed. It was sent to Luther who wrote, 'It pleases me right well and I do not know what to improve or change in it; neither would it be proper, for I cannot tread so gently and quietly.' It is one of the great historic documents of the Christian Church and is known as the Augsburg Confession.

The Emperor had tried to persuade all the Protestant princes at Augsburg to join in the annual Corpus Christi

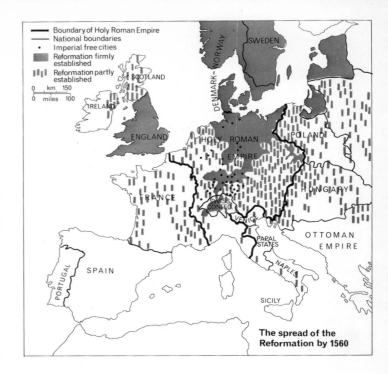

The spread of the Reformation by 1560

Boundary of Holy Roman Empire
National boundaries
Imperial free cities
Reformation firmly established
Reformation partly established

procession, but they refused. Discussions and conversations went on for many weeks between both sides to see if any agreement could be reached between the Protestants and the Catholics – but in vain. Finally, on 25 June, the spokesmen for two Protestant cities (Nuremberg and Reutlingen) and the princes of five Protestant states (Saxony, Hesse, Anhalt, Brandenburg–Ansbach, Brunswick–Lüneburg) signed the final form of the Augsburg Confession and gave it to the Emperor. The next day it was read aloud in German to the assembled Diet, so loudly that even the crowd outside could hear every word. It took two hours to read. Then more Protestant cities added their signatures.

John Eck – Luther's old opponent from the Leipzig debate – drew up the Catholic reply to the Confession and this reply was also read aloud. The Emperor then declared that the Protestants had been defeated by Eck's reply and he gave them one year in which to accept the Catholic teachings. He promised however to ask the Pope to call a general council of the whole Church to discuss the Protestants' criticisms. The Diet of

Luther's friend Philip Melanchthon, by Dürer, 1526. Melanchthon drew up the Augsburg Confession in 1530, setting out the beliefs of the Protestant reformers.

left: The Augsburg Confession is read aloud to the members of the Diet of Augsburg, 25 June 1530, in the presence of the Emperor Charles V.

Augsburg did not heal the split in the Church and did not give the Protestants what they had hoped. Henry VIII, who was King of England at that time, said that if only *he* had been at Augsburg he would have done a better job than Charles V and brought the two parties to an agreement! One thing the Diet did do was to bring the different Protestant groups closer together. They now could be clearly seen to be not just the followers of one rebellious monk but a whole Church whose members could speak with one voice. In 1531 the Protestant rulers formed the League of Schmalkalden. Germany now broke into two parts – a Catholic part and a Protestant part. Religious issues became more and more entangled with political issues. After years of squabbling, fighting and treachery, it became obvious that neither side could crush the other.

The Peace of Augsburg, 1555

Only in 1555 did the Protestants at last get part of what they were asking for at the Diet of 1530. It was set out in a document called the Peace of Augsburg and it said that the prince of each

state could decide whether he wanted to be a Protestant or a Catholic and his people would have to follow his decision. Anyone who did not want to follow would have to go and live in some other state where there was a prince of his own religion. This led to thousands of refugees, both Protestant and Catholic, trailing from one part of Germany to another, looking for freedom to practise their religion. The Peace of Augsburg meant freedom of choice for the princes but not really for the people.

The end of Luther's life

From 1530 onwards Luther's own personal influence on the ever-widening Reformation movement was growing weaker, though he continued to influence what went on in his own part of Germany by a great flow of letters and pamphlets, some of them bitter and angry, some gentle and compassionate. In these last years he gave some of his finest lectures and sermons, but at the same time his hatred of the Pope became more obsessive and the tone of his anti-Catholic writings more violent. Even though Protestantism had spread to the Netherlands, Scandinavia, England, Scotland, Switzerland and Bohemia, the power of Luther's enemies seemed to be growing. By the 1540s the Pope had called a council of the Church and the Emperor was beginning to assemble armies. The Counter-Reformation was gathering strength.

'I am an old, tired, chilled, frozen man', Luther said. He was often ill; he quarrelled bitterly with some of his former supporters; he grumbled about his students. What disappointed him most now that he was old was that Wittenberg itself had not become the community of Christian brotherly love he had hoped for. Callousness and immorality still persisted and all Luther's attempts to reform the people's way of life seemed to have failed. He felt his people were ungrateful for what he had done and he even left Wittenberg for a while in protest. All these disappointments made him very difficult to live with at the end of his life but he still kept the love and admiration of his friends and he never let go his simple trusting faith in God.

Early in 1546 he travelled to Eisleben, the town where he had been born sixty-two years before, to settle a local dispute between the Counts of Mansfeld. His wife was very anxious about him when he was away from her and she must have written him many of her worried letters. 'Don't be troubled', he wrote back to her, 'I have a better Protector than thou and all the angels. He it is who lay in a manger and was fondled on a maiden's breast, but was at the same time seated on the right hand of God the Almighty Father. Therefore be at peace.'

While he was at Eisleben Luther caught a chill and he died there on 18 February 1546. His friend Philip Melanchthon broke the news to the students in Wittenberg. He likened Luther to Elijah, the great prophet of the Old Testament. 'Alas', he said, 'gone is the horseman and the chariots of Israel.'

This photograph shows Luther's grave (front left) in the Wittenberg castle church where he so often preached in his lifetime. On the wall at the back is a memorial portrait of the reformer.

Index

Acknowledgments

The author and publisher wish to thank the following for permission to reproduce illustrations:

Pages 4, 5 (Cranach painting), 6, 9, 16, 33 (portrait), 34, 35, 38, 44, 48, Klaus G. Beyer; pp. 5 (Grünewald), 10, 14 (Creation), 21, 47 (Melanchthon), Mansell Collection; pp. 5 (woodcut), 15, 22, 23, 28, 29, 39, 40, Lutherhalle Reformationgeschichtliches Museum, Wittenberg; p. 7, Oeffentliche Kunstsammlung, Basel; p. 8 (reliquary), Fitzwilliam Museum, Cambridge; pp. 8 (pilgrims), 13 (Rome), 17, 27, 30 (title page), 31, 36, 42, 45, Cambridge University Library; pp. 11, 37 (cartoon), Germanisches Nationalmuseum, Nürnberg; pp. 13 (portrait), 24, 41, Staatliche Museen Preussischer Kulturbesitz, Berlin; p. 14 (pilgrims), Staatsgemäldesammlungen, Munich; pp. 19, 25, 26, 30 (woodcut), 31, 32, 37 (iconoclasts), Bodleian Library, Oxford; p. 43, Fürstlich Waldburg-Zeil'sches Archiv Schloss Zeil, Foto-Wagner; p. 47 (Confession), Bibliothèque Nationale, Paris.

The author and the publisher would also like to thank Erik Routley for supplying 'Ein' feste Burg' in modern notation, and Nicholas Boyle for the translation on page 22. The author also wishes to acknowledge her debt to the work of many Luther scholars and in particular to Professor E. Gordon Rupp for his kind advice and encouragement.

The picture on the front and back covers shows Martin Luther addressing the members of the Imperial Diet at Worms on 18 April 1521. Luther's lawyer, Professor Schurpff, stands beside him in the centre of the crowded, torch-lit room. The young Emperor, Charles V, is seated with his advisers on the right. Speaking first in Latin and then in German, Luther says: 'My conscience is captive to the Word of God. Therefore I cannot and I will not recant since it is neither safe nor right to go against one's conscience. God help me. Amen.'

Cover illustration by Graham Humphreys

The Cambridge History Library

The Cambridge Introduction to History
Written by Trevor Cairns

The Cambridge Topic Books
General Editor Trevor Cairns

The Cambridge History Library will be expanded in the future to include additional volumes. Lerner Publications Company is pleased to participate in making this excellent series of books available to a wide audience of readers.

Lerner Publications Company
241 First Avenue North, Minneapolis, Minnesota 55401